W9-BZV-014

MEXICO
Leading the Southern Hemisphere

Ancient Land with a Fascinating Past
The History of Mexico

An ancient statue watches over the El Castillo pyramid in Yucatán. Mexico's history has seen the rise and fall of many unique civilizations.

MEXICO
Leading the Southern Hemisphere

ANCIENT LAND WITH A
FASCINATING PAST
THE HISTORY OF MEXICO

MC **MASON CREST**
PHILADELPHIA

Mason Crest
450 Parkway Drive, Suite D
Broomall, PA 19008
www.masoncrest.com

Printed and bound in the United States of America.

CPSIA Compliance Information: Batch #M2014.
For further information, contact Mason Crest at 1-866-MCP-Book.

First printing
1 3 5 7 9 8 6 4 2

Library of Congress Cataloging-in-Publication Data
        on file at the Library of Congress

        ISBN: 978-1-4222-3218-7 (hc)
        ISBN: 978-1-4222-8683-8 (ebook)

Mexico: Leading the Southern Hemisphere series ISBN: 978-1-4222-3213-2

TABLE OF CONTENTS

MEXICO
Leading the Southern Hemisphere

KEY ICONS TO LOOK FOR:

 Text-dependent questions: These questions send the reader back to the text for more careful attention to the evidence presented there.

 Words to understand: These words with their easy-to-understand definitions will increase the reader's understanding of the text, while building vocabulary skills.

 Series glossary of key terms: This back-of-the book glossary contains terminology used throughout this series. Words found here increase the reader's ability to read and comprehend higher-level books and articles in this field.

 Research projects: Readers are pointed toward areas of further inquiry connected to each chapter. Suggestions are provided for projects that encourage deeper research and analysis.

 Sidebars: This boxed material within the main text allows readers to build knowledge, gain insights, explore possibilities, and broaden their perspectives by weaving together additional information to provide realistic and holistic perspectives.

TIMELINE

1000 B.C.	The Olmec civilization becomes a leader in development of writing, numbering, and astronomy.
400 B.C.	Olmec civilization disappears.
150 B.C.	Teotihuacán is built.
A.D. 750	Teotihuacán is abandoned.
300-900	Peak cultural growth of the Maya.
900-1200	Toltecs control much of Mexico.
1200	Aztecs begin to conquer other tribes for control of Mexico.
1325	Aztecs build Tenochtitlán.
1500	Aztecs control all land in central Mexico.
1517	Córdoba and Grijalva explore the coast of Mexico.
1521	Spanish take control of Mexico.
1810	Grito de Dolores calls for Mexico's independence from Spain.
1821	The Treaty of Córdoba grants Mexico its independence.
1810–1821	Mexican War of Independence is fought against Spain.
1862	France invades Mexico.
1867	Benito Juárez triumphs over the French, executes the Emperor Maximilian, and resumes his presidency.
1876	Porfirio Díaz begins his period of dictatorship.
1910	The Mexican Revolution begins.
1921	The end of the Revolution and the beginning of modern-day Mexico.

1938	President Cárdenas nationalizes the petroleum industry and takes control of Mexico's oil reserves.
1965	The Mexican government launches the Border Industrialization Program, which encourages the creation of small factories called maquiladoras.
1968	Mexico hosts the Summer Olympic Games, and violence breaks out during a student protest.
1994	The North American Free Trade Agreement (NAFTA) goes into effect in January.
2000	Vicente Fox, a PAN candidate, is elected president.
2006	The United States begins to construct a controversial fence along the border to reduce drug smuggling and illegal immigration. In December, Mexican president Felipe Calderón orders federal soldiers and police to intervene in turf wars among powerful drug cartels, beginning a period of violence known as the narco war.
2009	The Mexican government reports that more than 6,500 people were killed in drug-related incidents during the year, making it the deadliest year of the narco war.
2012	Enrique Peña Nieto is elected president of Mexico, receiving 38 percent of the vote. His election returns the PRI to power after 12 years of PAN rule. He is sworn in as president on December 1.
2014	Joaquin "El Chapo" Guzman, leader of the powerful Sinaloa drug cartel, is arrested by the Mexican military.

WORDS TO UNDERSTAND

conquistadors—the Spanish conquerors of the New World.

Mesoamerica—name for an area that stretches from modern-day central Mexico south to Honduras and Nicaragua. Before the arrival of Spanish conquistadors in the 16th century, many Amerindian civilizations flourished in this region.

No one is certain what these colossal heads are meant to represent. They were carved by the ancient Olmec people of Mexico. Most experts think these heads are meant to depict powerful Olmec kings, but because of the headgear some believe they may represent ballplayers or warriors.

1

ANCIENT CIVILIZATIONS

The first civilization to inhabit Mexico was probably the Olmecs. Historians believe that the Olmec civilization originated around 1500 B.C. These people were once thought to have settled in the Southern Coastal Plains, but the discovery of new ruins suggests that they may have originally settled on the Pacific Coast and moved inland.

The Olmec civilization is perhaps best known for making the "Olmec heads." These were large sculptures made of stone, depicting the heads of men wearing helmets. These sculptures were set at important Olmec sites, and are lasting reminders of this ancient culture.

The Olmecs are credited with developing a system of numbering, a calendar, and writing. They are believed to be the first people in the New World to develop religious centers and pyramids. These accomplishments earned them the title "mother culture" for the generations of Amerindian civilizations that followed in *Mesoamerica*. Despite all of the advances made by the Olmec culture, however, by 400 B.C., the Olmecs had disappeared. They were replaced by other civilizations, such as the Zapotec and the Mixtec.

The culture of all these ancient Mesoamerican civilizations still plays an important role in Mexico, for it continues to influence the art and culture of today's Mexicans. Mexican artists draw inspiration from these ancient roots, and the food, the language, and even the games that Mexicans enjoy all contain echoes from these long-ago ancestors.

But other new cultures arose in Mexico. The Maya were the most influential culture in Mesoamerica from about A.D. 250 to 900. During the peak of their power, their empire stretched throughout the Mexican states of Chiapas, Tabasco, Campeche, Yucatán, and Quintana Roo. They even extended into what are now the countries of Guatemala, Belize, and Honduras.

Another culture at this time was the Totonac civilization. These people built the city of El Tajín, which flourished from about A.D. 600 to 1200. They lived on the east coast of Mexico and in the mountains, and shared many similarities with the Maya, with whom they probably traded and occasionally fought against.

People of all cultures apparently lived together at Teotihuacán, one of the earliest and largest cities to develop in ancient Mexico. Located in the Valley of Mexico, Teotihuacán was a cultural and economic center of Mesoamerica. Eight miles square, the city was filled with large pyramids, wide streets, and a variety of shops and religious

The Olmecs are thought to be the original inventors of the game *tlachtli*, although later cultures like the Aztecs also played this game. The game is played on a court shaped like a capital H. Two sides compete, attempting to knock the ball into the opponent's side of the court. Although the contestants wore heavy padding, serious injury and even death resulted in some of these competitions. Nevertheless it was considered an exciting sport for nobles to watch and usually a good deal of betting took place on the outcome of the game.

Tourists walk through one of the main streets in Teotihuacán. The structure at the end of the avenue is the Pyramid of the Moon, which was built around A.D. 400.

centers. There even appear to have been apartment complexes. At its peak, 125,000 people lived in Teotihuacán. The members of this civilization had their own systems of writing and mathematics. Teotihuacán began to decline around A.D. 650 and was abandoned entirely by A.D. 750. Scholars are still not sure why the city was abandoned, although it appears that droughts and crop failures may have led the population to turn on its leaders and destroy religious sites.

From A.D. 900 to the arrival of the Spanish early in the 16th century, war was a constant feature of Mexican culture. While priests and other religious leaders had ruled earlier cultures, military kings began to take control of the various groups of Indians. The different groups struggled among themselves for control of the land and people.

The Toltecs were the next tribe to establish a large empire in Mexico. Between A.D. 900 and 1200, the Toltecs controlled land from Hidalgo north to Zacatecas, south to Guatemala, and east to the pyramids of Chichén Itzá. An uneasy peace existed between the Zapotecs and Mixtecs of Oaxaca, the Tarascans of Michoacán, and the Huastecs of northeast Mexico. The capital city of their empire was Tula, in the present-day state of Hidalgo.

Ruins of a ball court in the Mayan city of Uxmal. The ancient people of Mesoamerica played a ballgame that required players to put the ball through a stone hoop to score. The games were often part of a larger ritual that probably included human sacrifice.

Sculptures of Toltec warriors at the city of Tula. The Toltec culture appears to have been centered on fighting so soldiers had an important place. Tula was eventually conquered and destroyed around A.D. 1200.

When the Aztecs arrived from the north, they admired the Toltecs and viewed them as their predecessors. The Aztecs arrived in Mexico as "savages," but they quickly adopted the customs and practices of other Amerindian civilizations. Soon, the Aztecs were improving methods of agriculture and building that had been developed by the Maya and Toltec peoples.

In 1325 the Aztecs began to build Tenochtitlán, their new capital. The Aztecs formed an alliance with the Tepanec people. First, the Aztecs served as the Tepanecs' warriors, but eventually, by 1428, the Aztecs overthrew the Tepanecs and seized control of the Valley of Mexico for themselves.

The legend of the Aztecs says that the god of war led them south from their original home. Where they saw an eagle perched on a cactus with a snake in its beak, they were to build their new capital. This is where they constructed their city of Tenochtitlán, which is also the site of modern-day Mexico City.

This mural depicting Aztec life is displayed in the Palacio Nacional in Mexico City. The Aztecs built a powerful civilization during the 15th century. Today, however, few of their customs are reflected in Mexican life.

By 1500, the Aztecs controlled all the lands and people of central Mexico. Aztec warriors believed that they were destined to die in battle. According to their beliefs, upon their death they would become hummingbirds and fly to the sun. Their lack of fear while doing battle helped them to achieve rapid and total control of central Mexico. The tribes the Aztecs conquered had to pay tribute and taxes in the form of precious stones, metals, feathers, and food.

By the arrival of the Spanish *conquistadors* in 1519, the Aztecs were the dominant empire of Middle America. Nahuatl, the language of the Aztecs, was spoken from Panama to western North America. Nahuatl is still spoken by Indians in several parts of Mexico today.

TEXT-DEPENDENT QUESTIONS

What was one of the earliest and largest cities to develop in ancient Mexico?

Which ancient Mesoamerican civilization did the Aztec people most admire?

RESEARCH PROJECT

Create a replica of an Olmec head, using modeling clay. Refer to the photo on page 10 of this book, or search the Internet for other images to use as a guide. Include the headgear and distinctive facial features.

 WORDS TO UNDERSTAND

asset—an advantage or resource.

armada—a fleet of Spanish warships.

crossbows—a weapon made by setting a short bow crosswise at the end of a beam used to shoot square-headed bolts or arrows.

rigging—the lines and chains used on a ship to support and move the sails and masts.

smallpox—a contagious disease that causes high fevers and pus-filled sores that leave deep scars.

2

In this 17th century painting, the Aztec emperor Montezuma II bows in respect to Hernán Cortés. The surprising victory of a handful of Spanish conquistadors over the vast Aztec empire helped to shape Mexico's history for several hundred years.

THE SPANISH ARRIVE

I n the late 15th century, Spain was just emerging as a united country of Europe. In 1492, the Spanish rulers King Ferdinand and Queen Isabella sent Christopher Columbus on a mission to find a trade route to China by sailing west across the Atlantic Ocean. Columbus instead landed on islands in the Caribbean, including Cuba, which until that time were unknown to Europeans. On subsequent voyages Columbus explored other islands, as well as the coast of South America. Spain soon claimed ownership of all the lands in this "New World," and set out to explore the lands and exploit their resources.

The Spaniards established a colony on Cuba in 1511, naming Diego Velázquez as governor. Velázquez's first task was to kill or enslave the local Amerindians, to ensure the colony would survive. Once this was done, in April 1518 he sent an expedition commanded by Francisco Hernández de Córdoba and Juan de Grijalva to explore the region further. They returned to Cuba with reports of massive wealth and population along the Yucatán peninsula. Late in 1518, Velázquez appointed Hernán Cortés to lead a military force into the unknown land. Cortés left in February 1519 with 11 small ships, carrying about 550 soldiers and 16 horses.

Representatives of Montezuma, the Aztec king, greeted the Spaniards soon after they landed. Believing the Spaniards to be gods, the Aztecs provided Cortés and his men with gold and other valuables as gifts. They were hoping that the Spanish would take the gifts and leave, but their plan backfired. Cortés became convinced that this was a chance to win glory in Spain, and he decided to conquer this new land. Afraid that his men might abandon him, he burned his ships as a way to communicate that there was no going back. They were in this new land to stay.

Cortés established the city of Veracruz on the coast of Mexico and appointed one of his soldiers as governor. This governor then granted Cortés permission to conquer the New World and claim it as Spain's.

 Friar Bartolomé de las Casas arrived in New Spain in 1531. He recognized that the Spaniards were not treating the Indians fairly and worked tirelessly to defend them. In his position as a king-appointed missionary, he wrote a book condemning the Spaniards' treatment of the Indians; the book was published and read in Europe. He worked for the fair and equal treatment of Indians until his death in 1566. Although his work did not directly provide equal treatment of the Indians, it opened the eyes of many Europeans to the atrocities happening in the New World.

It seemed like an impossible task. Cortés had just a few hundred soldiers, while the Aztec kingdom consisted of over 5 million people and dozens of city-states in addition to the capital at Tenochtitlán. However, the Spaniards had several advantages. The Aztecs believed that the Spaniards were gods, and that their arrival had been predicted in religious stories. The Spaniards' were also armed with *crossbows*, armor, cannons, and swords. Perhaps the Spaniards' greatest *asset* was the smoldering hatred that many other native groups felt for the Aztec rulers.

Hernán Cortés was able to conquer the powerful Aztecs in part because they treated him with reverence at first, believing he was a god.

Having been forced to pay tribute to Tenochtitlán for many years, many of the Amerindian tribes were willing to help Cortés and his men defeat the Aztecs. One tribe that lived on the Gulf Coast provided Cortés with Doña Marina, a young Indian woman who acted as translator and advisor to Cortés. With her help, Cortés was able to determine the weaknesses of the Aztecs, as well as convince many Amerindians to join the side of the Spaniards.

Cortés's first strategy for doing battle with the Aztecs was to approach Tenochtitlán along the narrow causeway that extended through the lake on which the city was built. Montezuma, expecting Cortés and his men to be friendly, invited them into the fortress. The Spaniards lived in the palace for months, and eventually imprisoned Montezuma. The Aztecs became upset that the Spanish army was living in their city, and soon a bloody battle ensued. Cortés and the Spaniards were forced to retreat from Tenochtitlán. Many Spaniards were killed. Montezuma himself may have been killed in the confusion, possibly by the Aztecs themselves.

Cortés realized that he would not be able to use the narrow strip of land to approach Tenochtitlán again. He decided to gather all the sails and *rigging* from the remains of the ships the Spaniards had arrived on, and sent his men to cut lumber in the forests. Reinforcements of supplies and horses arrived

The Spaniards were disgusted by the religious rituals of the Aztecs, especially those involving human sacrifice. They banned these practices and forced natives to convert to Christianity.

from Cuba while Cortés was making his preparations. With the help of over 8,000 friendly Amerindians, these materials were carried over the mountains to the shore of the lake surrounding Tenochtitlán. Cortés then began the construction of a small *armada*, with the idea of waging a water attack on the unsuspecting Aztecs. By April 1521, Cortés had assembled 13 warships with cannons, a fleet of canoes with armed Indians, over 900 armed Spanish soldiers, including 84 horsemen, and thousands of Indian warriors on foot.

But the biggest asset that Cortés had was *smallpox* and other diseases. Before the arrival of the Spaniards, the natives had never been exposed to these illnesses. They soon became sick, and that, combined with the Spaniards cutting off their food and water supply, caused a serious situation for the Indians. Once Cuauhtémoc, the new Aztec king, was captured, the Aztec capital soon fell. On August 13, 1521, barely 90 days into the battle, the Spaniards conquered Tenochtitlán.

The Spaniards established a new city on the ruins of Tenochtitlán, and began calling the territory New Spain. Cortés sent his men out to explore New Spain and conquer the remaining Amerindian tribes.

Cortés and his men believed that the Aztecs were preparing to stage a revolt, with Cuauhtémoc's encouragement. In 1524, Cuauhtémoc, who was still being held as a prisoner of the Spaniards, was executed. With the Aztecs totally defeated, by 1525 the Spanish colony of New Spain had expanded southward to include land that is part of present-day Guatemala and Honduras. The Mayan Indians proved to be the most difficult

Quetzalcoatl was considered the wisest and most kind of the Aztec gods. In most drawings he was depicted as having a beard. According to Aztec legend, Quetzalcoatl was forced out of his land by another god. He promised that he would return in the year that the Europeans numbered as 1519. During that year, a messenger arrived in Tenochtitlán and told Montezuma of strange men with light skin and facial hair. Their appearance on the shore of Mexico, seemingly from nowhere, along with the horses they brought, which the Aztecs had never seen, convinced Montezuma of one thing: Quetzalcoatl had returned. Based on this assumption, Montezuma and his men accommodated Cortés and his men, offering gifts and inviting them into their fortress. This was a deadly mistake. With such an advantage, it is no wonder that Cortés was able to defeat the Aztecs so easily.

The excavated remains of the Templo Mayor, one of the main Aztec temples in Tenochtitlán. The temple was destroyed by the Spanish when they conquered the city in 1521. The current capital of Mexico, Mexico City, was built on the ruins of Tenochtitlán.

for the Spanish to conquer. They retained control of the Yucatán peninsula for another 20 years or more and remained independent in some areas of Mexico for over 150 years.

The Spaniards spent a great deal of time expanding their settlements to the north, where rich deposits of gold and silver were located. Franciscan and Jesuit priests were among the first permanent settlers in the area. Through the development of mission fortresses, the priests worked to convert the Indians to the Catholic faith and discourage them from raiding the silver and

With no immunity to the diseases that the Spanish brought with them, Native Americans died in great numbers. The poor treatment that they received as slaves to their Spanish master also caused many deaths. From 1519 to 1700, the population of Indians dropped from over 25 million to around 1 million.

25

gold and mines that the Spaniards constructed. When the Spaniards could not convert the natives to their faith willingly, they resorted to military force. Relationships with the Indians were strained, largely due to the Spaniards' enslavement of them. In 1537 the Catholic pope officially discouraged slavery in the colony, but ill will remained.

TEXT-DEPENDENT QUESTIONS

What city on the coast of Mexico did Cortés use as a base for his conquest of the Aztecs? Who was the Aztec ruler that succeeded Montezuma?

RESEARCH PROJECT

In the Spanish colonies of the New World, including Cuba and New Spain (Mexico), the Spaniards implemented a system called encomendia. The Spanish king granted control over land to reward a valued follower; along with the land came the Native Americans who lived there, as well as any resources contained there. The person who received the grant, known as an encomendero, was responsible for instructing the natives in the Roman Catholic faith. In return, they were expected to work for the encomendero. Find out more about the encomendia system, and write a report. Explain how was it was similar to/different from slavery, and what the advantages and disadvantages were for both the Spanish and for the Native Americans.

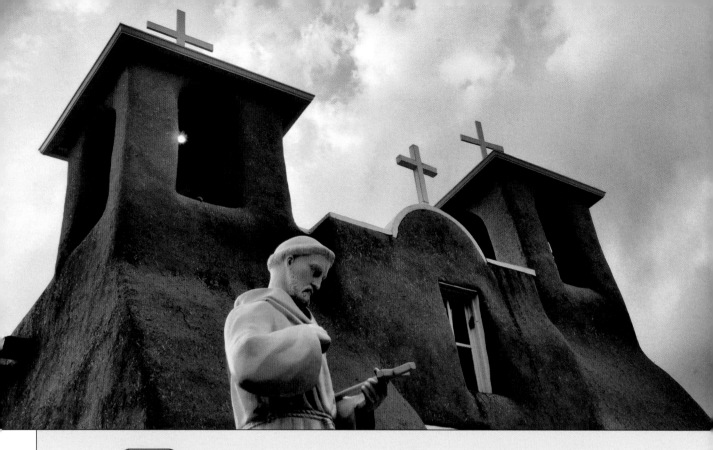

WORDS TO UNDERSTAND

civil—having to do with citizens; a civil war is fought between citizens of the same country.

colonialism—control of one power or nation over a dependent area or people.

democracy—the system of government where the people of the country elect their leaders to represent their interests.

exports—products or commodities that are shipped out of a country.

3

Spanish rulers believed it was their responsibility to spread Christianity to as many souls as possible. In order to achieve this, they built missions throughout New Spain, where Roman Catholic priests and religious leaders could teach the natives.

INDEPENDENCE FOR MEXICO

By 1600, Spain controlled most of what is now Mexico. Governing this vast area was proving to be very difficult, however. The distance from Europe as well as the unhappiness of the general population led to many problems.

Missionaries established most of the governments of New Spain. In the 16th century, these missionaries built, with the help of Indians who had converted to Christianity, over 100,000 churches and convents. The churches acted as local governments in most areas of New Spain. By three centuries later, the Catholic Church owned over half of the buildings in Mexico. Church property was not taxed, so Spain did not enjoy the wealth that was developing in New Spain at this time.

New Spain also spent a great deal of time and effort developing its silver mines. During this period of **colonialism**, the world's production of silver doubled, thanks to **exports** from New Spain. The Spanish settlers also developed *haciendas*, or large ranches. The wealth of New Spain rested mainly with a small group of *criollos* that owned these haciendas and silver mines. Criollos were pureblooded Spaniards who were born in New Spain.

But Spanish law prevented criollos from holding political office. At the time only *gachupines*, or Spaniards actually born in Spain, were permitted to become officials. This caused much resentment among the criollos. Growing populations of Spanish-Indians, known as *mestizos*, were also becoming impatient with the Spaniards' treatment of Indians.

While the American and French Revolutions were being fought, many settlers of New Spain began to question the government. The world was full of new ideas about government and ***democracy***, and people in New Spain began to take a fresh look at how they wanted to live. Anger at the oppression of the Indians combined with the criollos' desire for free trade with countries other than Spain; the combination caused a number of unlikely allies. As a result, many of the priests gathered criollos on their side and declared their desire for independence from Spain.

In 1804, King Charles III of Spain ordered that all church funds should be given to Spain. Since the churches had acted as banks for the criollos, this caused tremendous problems for many of the people of New Spain.

The plans for revolution might have fallen apart, however, if not for Napoléon Bonaparte. Bonaparte had taken control of France, and

José María Morelos, a priest who strongly agreed with the revolution, took up the challenge of leadership after fellow priest Miguel Hidalgo was executed. Morelos had spent the early years of his priesthood working with mestizos and Indians. He joined with Hidalgo in 1811, and after Hidalgo's death he fought tirelessly for the revolution. In 1813 he drafted the Congress of Chilpancingo. This document was the basis for a constitution. In November of the same year, the rebels declared independence from Spain. Spanish forces soon caught up with Morelos and his men, and Morelos was shot as a traitor.

The policies of Spanish king Charles III, who is shown in this painting by Francisco José de Goya y Lucientes, caused many problems for the people of Mexico, or New Spain, as the colony was known at that time. When he financially drained the churches of New Spain, Mexico was ready to fight for independence.

Napoléon Bonaparte was a French general whose main goal was the expansion of France through the conquest of Europe. King Charles the IV of Spain fell into disfavor with the Spanish people by allowing Bonaparte to occupy Lisbon. As King Charles the IV prepared to abdicate the throne to his son, Ferdinand VII, Napoléon decided that he should end Spanish rule entirely. In 1808 he forced King Charles and Ferdinand to abdicate, and appointed Joseph Bonaparte to rule Spain. The Spanish people disliked this, and through a violent upheaval, they drove Napoléon and his men out of Spain and Portugal. This was the beginning of the end of Napoléon's conquest of Europe.

when he sought to extend his power into Spain in 1808, his invasion caused the Spanish king a great deal of hardship. Struggling to retain control of Spain, the Spanish government had few resources left to deal with New Spain. The conditions were ripe for revolution.

On September 16, 1810, a priest from the city of Dolores issued a proclamation calling for the end of Spanish rule. Miguel Hidalgo y Costilla had long been troubled by the oppression of Native Americans. He was a friend of the Indians, teaching them farming methods and pottery. Under Spanish rule, this was illegal, and the viceroy of New Spain planned to arrest him. In response, Hidalgo issued his *Grito de Dolores* (Cry of Dolores), calling for self-rule, equality among the different groups living in New Spain, and redistribution of land from the wealthy to the poor. This marked the beginning of the revolt.

A leader of the criollos who was planning to overthrow the gachupines was Ignacio Allende. Allende, a former officer in the Spanish army, was a main force in the criollos' fight for freedom. When he heard that Hidalgo was to be arrested, he joined forces with the priest. The two men hoped to avoid a battle with Spain by convincing the army to support them rather than the gachupines. The men gathered supporters of criollos, mestizos, and Indians, and moved into Mexico City.

Despite the leaders' peaceful intentions, the years of mistreatment at the hands of the Spaniards had taken their toll. Once the rebellion had the government in its sight, a bloody battle ensued. Despite early victory, the viceroy managed to squash the rebellion in 1811. Hidalgo and Allende were executed, but new leaders emerged from this battle, and *civil* war and revolution would continue for 75 more years.

A statue of Father Miguel Hidalgo, one of the important leaders of the Mexican War for Independence.

The continual battles took their toll on the governments and people of New Spain. Soon the gachupine leaders began to desire freedom from Spain as well. Their desire for freedom was more self-serving, however, since they actually

Agustín de Iturbide helped to draft the Plan de Iguala, and led a triumphant revolutionary army into Mexico City in 1821. Iturbide became emperor of Mexico that year, but his government soon collapsed.

hoped to gain more wealth and power by becoming independent. They united secretly with the revolutionaries and drafted the *Plan de Iguala*. The plan declared Mexico an independent nation. Its inhabitants were to be equal, whether they were from European or native descent. Spain, thousands of miles

José María Morelos was a revolutionary Catholic priest who received the title of Generalissimo of the Mexican Army. Though he was executed by the Spanish, his determination was revered and exemplified by the Mexican people.

away, did not see any way to refuse the proposition, and the plan was signed in 1821. One provision that Spain made was that a representative from the Spanish government head the new government in Mexico City. By the time this representative arrived from Spain, however, the new Mexican government had united and forced him to sign the Treaty of Córdoba. This treaty, signed by the king's representative, Juan O'Donojú, on August 24, 1821, ended Spain's involvement in New Spain.

TEXT-DEPENDENT QUESTIONS
What French leader helped to create the conditions for the war for independence from Spain? Who helped to draft the Plan de Iguala?

RESEARCH PROJECT
On September 18, Mexicans celebrate the "Grito de Dolores," a declaration of independence shouted by Father Miguel Hidalgo in the small town of Dolores, near Guanajuato, in 1810. This event marked the beginning of the Mexican War of Independence. Using the Internet or your school library, find out more about Father Hidalgo. Write a one-page report about Hidalgo's life and his influence on the movement for independence.

Statue depicting a Mexican cowboy traveling with a herd of cattle in Aguascalientes.

4

UNREST CONTINUES IN MEXICO

Mexico's independence from Spain was only the beginning of a violent period of internal and external struggle. One group in Mexico wanted the nation to be ruled as a *republic*, while another group wanted it ruled as an *empire*. Initially the group that wanted an empire won, and Agustín de Iturbide was appointed ruler. However, his government lasted only two years before it was overthrown.

The new government established Mexico as a republic, the United States of Mexico. They drafted a new *constitution* in 1824, dividing the country into 19 states, four territories, and a federal district. The constitution also called for an end to slavery and granted all men the right to vote. Although a step in the right direction, severe restrictions in the laws made it impossible for the poorest citizens to vote. Unrest continued. The government, unstable from fighting and without many of the Spaniards who had grown wealthy in the mines and haciendas, was nearly broke. When the government could not pay the military's wages, the military seized control and created a new government.

This new government borrowed money from other countries to keep itself afloat. Instead of using the money to develop the country's resources, the money was spent to pay off the government's debt. As soon as that money was gone, another revolt occurred.

Agustín de Iturbide was the first leader of Mexico once the country won its independence from Spain. Responsible for the *Plan de Iguala*, which declared independence from Spain, guaranteed equality among the races, and stated that the Catholic Church would be the official church of Mexico, Iturbide was considered a military hero. Once he appointed himself ruler of Mexico, however, many of the people began to feel that rule by Iturbide would not be any better than rule by Spain. The Mexican people wanted their independence, and within two years Santa Anna had overthrown Iturbide. Iturbide abdicated the throne and moved to Europe. The next year he returned to Mexico, unaware that the government had called for his death. On July 19, 1824, Iturbide was executed. The Catholic Church still considers Iturbide a hero for the emphasis that he placed on the importance of the Catholic religion.

Antonio López de Santa Anna, an army general, was initially charged with ridding the country of Spaniards. As his ambition grew, he began seizing power. In 1824, he revoked the constitution. He appointed himself president and was in and out of office 11 times between 1833 and 1855.

As Americans began settling in northern Mexico, they talked of establishing their own country, independent of Mexico. By 1834, the Americans outnumbered the Mexicans in the northern part of Mexico. In 1835, these settlers declared their independence. Santa Anna attacked the Americans at the Alamo, defeating them soundly. At a later battle in San Jacinto, however, the Americans defeated the Mexicans and captured Santa Anna. Santa Anna was forced to sign the Velasco Agreement in 1836, giving northern Mexico its freedom.

Mexico, furious over this loss, *exiled* Santa Anna and refused to recognize the

Antonio López de Santa Anna was a Mexican soldier, president, and dictator. Though he was a respected military man, his troops suffered a sound defeat at the battle of San Jacinto. This misstep led to the loss of a large chunk of northern Mexico, which later became part of the United States as the state of Texas.

Velasco Agreement. For nine years, this area in northern Mexico was in limbo. It considered itself a free state, but Mexico still considered it part of the country. Finally, the United States admitted the land into the Union, and it became the state of Texas.

This caused Mexico to declare war on the United States. The Mexican government reconciled with Santa Anna, and asked him to lead the war against the United States. The United States troops were led by General Zachary Taylor, and they were much better prepared for battle than the Mexican

American troops prepare to attack the stronghold at Mexican City in 1847. Mexico lost roughly half of its territory in the Mexican-American War.

The Treaty of Guadalupe Hidalgo ended the Mexican War, at a vast sacrifice of Mexican land. The United States gained 1,193,061 square miles to its territory through this agreement, including New Mexico and California.

troops. American forces captured Mexico City on September 14, 1847; the Mexican-American war was officially over on February 2, 1848, when the Treaty of Guadalupe Hidalgo was signed. This treaty called for Mexico to turn over all land north of the Río Grande River (Texas), as well as all the land from the Gila River to the Pacific Ocean (what is now California, Nevada, Utah, and Arizona, as well as parts of Wyoming, Colorado, and New Mexico).

Despite Santa Anna's military failures, Mexico allowed him to name himself dictator of Mexico. In order to raise funds for the military, he sold additional land to the United States. In 1854 he sold a piece of Mexico along the Gila River (present-day Arizona and New Mexico) to the United States for $10 million. This deal, called the Gadsden Purchase, was the last major change of Mexican boundary lines. Mexico had lost over 50 percent of its territory to the United States in just a few short years.

Santa Anna was removed from power for the final time in 1855. Benito Juárez was appointed minister of justice and began a process of reform and rebuilding. Juárez was a strong believer in the anticlerical movement, which sought to

Benito Pablo Juárez was born to Zapotec Indian parents in Oaxaca. He went on to twice be elected president of his country. His main goal was to apply some degree of reform to the tumultuous government of Mexico.

make the Catholic Church less important to the economy. A new constitution was drafted in 1857, but three years of battles passed before Juárez and his men were able to capture and maintain control of Mexico City. Juárez was named president of Mexico and began efforts to rebuild the nation's economy.

During this rebuilding stage, Mexico quit making payments on loans from England, Spain, and France. Although Juárez tried to assure the countries that this was only a temporary situation until the economy of Mexico was stabilized, the countries, on the advice of the conservative government that Juárez had overthrown, sent warships to Mexico.

While England and Spain only wanted their money, France, ruled at the time by Napoléon III, nephew of Napoléon Bonaparte, thought this would be an opportunity to expand France's power into the New World. England and Spain quickly withdrew their troops, but France invaded Mexico on May 5, 1862. Initially, Mexico was able to hold off the assault, but on June 10, 1863, Mexico City was captured. Juárez was forced to go into hiding in northern Mexico.

In 1864, Napoléon appointed Maximilian, archduke of Austria, as the emperor of Mexico. Unwelcome by the Mexicans, Maximilian had a difficult time establishing an effective government in Mexico. Finally, after the American Civil War ended, the United States became interested in driving France out of Mexico. Between the pressure applied by the United States and problems in France, including the threat of an invasion by Prussia, Napoléon soon withdrew his troops from Mexico and returned to France.

But Maximilian refused to return to Europe when Napoléon withdrew his troops. He had worked hard for the interests of the Mexican people, and now he believed they wanted him to remain as leader. His wife, Carlota, traveled to Europe, seeking support for her husband. She went insane, however, and her husband was captured and executed by the Mexican troops soon after.

Juárez was reelected as president of Mexico, and he set about trying to strengthen the economy of Mexico. He created *infrastructure*, such as railroads and schools, and reduced the size of the military, which cost a considerable amount of money to operate.

In 1872, some army officials, led by a general by the name of Porfirio Díaz, attempted a *coup* on Juárez's government. This failed attempt was a sign of the unrest that was to come. Juárez died of a heart attack in 1873 and was succeeded by Sebastián Lerdo. Lerdo's reelection attempt in 1876 failed, and Porfirio Díaz became president of Mexico.

41

TEXT-DEPENDENT QUESTIONS

Which Mexican province declared its independence in 1835?

What is the Gadsden Purchase?

RESEARCH PROJECT

Find out about the Mexican-American War, waged from 1846 to 1848. Write a report explaining how this conflict affected Mexico as a nation, as well as how the invading American troops destabilized the Yucatán peninsula, leading to a lengthy native rebellion.

WORDS TO UNDERSTAND

guerrilla—a warfare technique involving surprise attacks and sabotage.

strikes—refusals to work in an attempt to gain better working conditions or higher pay.

5

FINAL REVOLUTION

Díaz was a ruthless dictator. Although relatively uneducated, he cared little for the plight of the poorer people of Mexico, and his rule was marked by the increased wealth of Mexico's upper class. He did not accept any questioning of his authority, and his government worked quickly to squash any protest by the Mexican citizens. Díaz created a police force known as the *Rurales*. The *Rurales* were given extreme latitude in what they were allowed to do, and they frequently used violence to maintain order.

Most of Díaz's rule resulted in no economic improvements for Mexico, but during his last 16 years in office, Díaz brought José Yves Limantour to Mexico to develop the economy. Limantour surrounded himself with well-educated men and worked tirelessly to build the treasury of Mexico. Foreign companies began to mine the nation's silver and gold and develop the oil deposits. By the end of Díaz's rule, foreign trade had increased 10 times from what it had been under Juárez's presidency.

From the outside, it appeared that Mexico was on a successful track, both economically and politically. Internally, things were not going so well. Wealthy landowners had acquired most of the land in Mexico, and the majority of the citizens worked for these landowners as little more than slaves. They were

Porfirio Díaz served as president from 1876 to 1880, and then from 1884 until 1911. This period of Mexican history is known as the Porfiriato.

forced to go into debt to the landowners; due to poor wages and unfair labor practices, they were then never able to rid themselves of the debt. The debt would even pass from one generation to the next.

In the cities, small political groups were emerging that were growing tired of Díaz's oppressive rule. This movement, known as *Regeneración* (Regeneration), staged **strikes** and peaceful protests. They resented the oppression caused by Díaz and wanted freedom for themselves and their fellow citizens. Díaz ruthlessly stopped these protests with deadly battles.

In 1910, Francisco Madero ran for president against Díaz. Díaz had Madero arrested and claimed victory in the election. When Madero was released from prison, he moved to the United States. From there, he began to plan a way to conquer Díaz. On November 20, 1910, Madero declared that the election was void and stated that the people of Mexico should stand up for their rights. Various small rebellions sprung up across Mexico. Díaz managed to resist most of these threats, but in the state of Chihuahua, a small group, led by Pancho Villa, managed to fend off Díaz's men. Madero joined forces with Villa and Pascual Orozco, and together they made a serious effort to gain control of

Mexico. Díaz, elderly and aware that he was losing power, resigned as president and moved to Paris.

Madero was elected president and immediately sought to prove his leadership. When Emiliano Zapata, a key figure in helping Madero drive Díaz from Mexico, asked Madero to return land that had been seized by Díaz, he refused. Zapata, Pancho Villa, and other former supporters now began to wage war against Madero and his government. Madero was arrested and shot by the group, and General Victoriano Huerta, who betrayed Madero and was responsible for his arrest, was named president. Huerta also did not want to return the seized land, and Zapata and Villa continued their *guerrilla* tactics.

The revolution might have lasted indefinitely had it not been for the intervention of the United States. Woodrow Wilson had been elected president of the United States in 1912, and he strongly supported the efforts of Mexican revolutionaries. He allowed the shipment of guns and ammunition to the rebels and sent troops to occupy Veracruz. With the United States on the side of the rebels, Huerta fled the country.

A battle for power ensued between Pancho Villa and Álvaro Obregón. Eventually many of Villa's men

Francisco Indalecio Madero was a Mexican revolutionary and politician who opposed Díaz in the 1910 presidential election. When Díaz relinquished power, Madero became president. However, some of his policies alienated supporters and Madero's government was overthown in 1913.

(Top) A group of armed men (insurrectos) during the 1910–1921 Mexican Revolution.

(Bottom) Three important leaders of the revolutionary period. (Left) Victoriano Huerta (1850–1916), a military officer who engineered the 1913 coup that overthrew Madero; (center) Venustiano Carranza (1859–1920), whose forces defeated Huerta and forced him to resign in 1914. Carranza subsequently became the first president of the Mexican republic; (Right) Álvaro Obregón (1880–1928), elected president in 1921, helped to restore order to Mexico after the destructive civil war.

were killed in battle with Plutarco Elías Calles. With Villa losing such an important battle, the United States withdrew its support and Venustiano Carranza was named president.

On February 5, 1917, Mexico adopted a new constitution, under the guidance of Carranza, and it is still used today. The new constitution reduced the power of the church and discouraged the hacienda system that had caused such inequality throughout Mexico. Although the new constitution stated that the government would provide for social and economic development of the people, in reality Carranza never fully adopted these proposals.

In 1920, Carranza was assassinated while trying to flee the country, and Obregón became president. His presidency, beginning in 1921, marked the end of the worst violence of the revolution, as well as the start of reform. Obregón focused on improving the Mexican school system and helping the Mexican people. This made him a popular leader.

TEXT-DEPENDENT QUESTIONS

In what state did Pancho Villa begin his resistance to Díaz's government?

What American president supported Mexican rebel groups against the Huerta regime?

RESEARCH PROJECT

A constitution is a collection of fundamental principles or guidelines that are used to govern a state. Mexico's current constitution was ratified in 1917. Find the Mexican constitution online (the text is available at http://www.juridicas.unam.mx/infjur/leg/constmex/pdf/consting.pdf) and read through it. What are some of the rights that the constitution promises to all Mexicans?

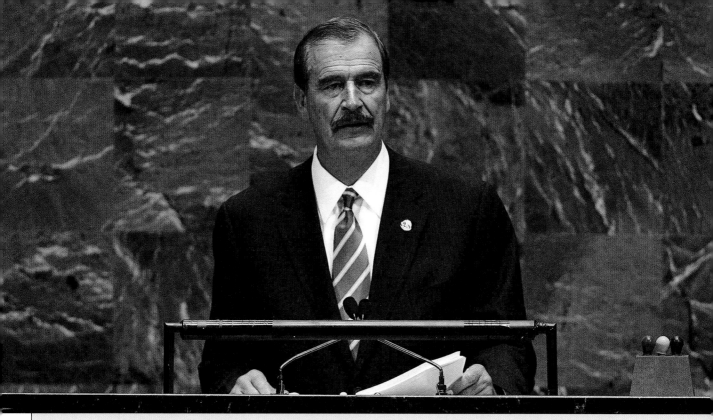

WORDS TO UNDERSTAND

bracero—from the Spanish term for "manual laborer," a Mexican who came to the U.S. seasonally for agricultural work.

illiterate—unable to read or write.

liberal—believing in progress and the protection of human rights; the opposite of conservative.

peso—the Mexican unit of money.

succeeded—followed; came next as an official or leader.

6

When Vicente Fox of the National Action Party (PAN) was sworn in as president of Mexico in December 2000, he became the first representative of a party other than the PRI to hold power in over 70 years. Fox served until 2006.

MODERN-DAY HOPES

Obregón's presidency lasted for four years, and his work to rebuild Mexico was appreciated by the people. Plutarco Elías Calles, who supported the constitution and ideals of Mexico, **succeeded** him. Unfortunately, the longer Calles was in power, the more dictatorial he became. He passed laws that were intended to weaken the power of the Roman Catholic church in Mexico. This led to a conflict between 1926 and 1929 called the Cristero War. Thousands of priests and Catholics were killed.

As the fighting continued at the end of his term, Calles had a plan to return Obregón to the presidency. However, soon after Obregón was reelected in 1928, he was assassinated by José de León Toral, who considered him responsible for the persecution of Roman Catholics. The next six years was a period that became known as the Maximato, in which Emilio Portes Gil, Pascual Ortiz Rubio, and Abelardo Rodríguez all served as president, but did Calles's bidding. During this time, the Partido Nacional Revolucionario (PNR) was formed. This was the beginning of a political party that still exists today, although it is now called the Partido Revolucionario Institucional (Institutional Revolutionary Party, or PRI).

In 1934, Lázaro Cárdenas became the PNR candidate for president, with the support of Calles. Once he was elected, Cárdenas began to strengthen the labor

After becoming president in 1934, Lázaro Cárdenas (1895–1970) transformed Mexico. He nationalized the oil industry and implemented land reforms.

movement within Mexico. Calles disagreed with this tactic, but Cárdenas was a popular leader. He eventually forced Calles to leave the country.

Cárdenas developed the Mexican election system that is still in use today. He also implemented an *ejido system* that helped to create peace within the country. Ejidos are lands that are jointly owned by a group of citizens. The ejidos typically consist of farmland, pastures, and a small township. Each family in the community has a section that they can work independently. This process works well, for most citizens cannot afford large areas of land privately; owned jointly and passed through generations of families, it is an affordable way to live. Even today, most rural land in Mexico is governed under the ejido system.

Cárdenas also masterminded the move that allowed Mexico to develop its economic independence. For many years foreign countries had developed the oil in Mexico, with Mexico not receiving any of the profits. In 1938, Cárdenas nationalized the oil industry and seized the foreign company's holdings. Britain was angered by the move, and the United States nearly considered declaring war on Mexico. Instead, due to negotiations between Cárdenas and President Franklin D. Roosevelt, Mexico agreed to pay for the land but retain the oil rights. It took

Mexico until 1962 to repay the debt of over $100 million, but once it did, the country was able to profit from the oil. The growth of the oil industry, as well as natural gas production and the development of factories led to growth in the middle class of Mexico.

Mexico helped the United States immensely during World War II. Mexicans came to the U.S. to work in factories and on farms. New laws allowed Mexican workers known as *braceros* to live in the U.S. during the growing season, and then return to Mexico when the harvest was complete. Some Mexicans also served in the military. After the war ended, the bracero program continued until the mid-1960s.

In 1965, a new form of economic help for Mexico arrived with the Border Industrialization Program. This allowed for the creation of small factories and assembly plants, called maquiladoras, which would provide much-needed jobs. The maquiladoras are assembly plants where the pieces of a product are imported into Mexico. The product is assembled in Mexico, then exported from Mexico to other markets around the world. Most

Mexican workers who were recruited by the U.S. Farm Security Administration to harvest and process sugar beets, 1943. During the Second World War there was a shortage of farm laborers, so Mexican workers were invited to help bring in the harvests.

The *Partido Revolucionario Nacional* (National Party of the Revolution) has been the dominant political party in Mexico since the 1920s. The party's name changed after World War II, and it became known as *Partido Revolucionario Institucional* (Institutional Revolutionary Party).

52

of these maquiladoras were located in Mexican states close to the U.S. border.

In the late 1960s, the Mexican government also began promoting tourism to improve the national economy. The government funded tourist resorts in places like Cancún and Acapulco. Today, Mexico is one of the most visited countries in the world.

During the 1970s the Mexican government borrowed money to fund tourism development and other projects. These loans nearly crippled the Mexican economy in the early 1980s, when the international price of oil dropped substantially. Mexico was unable to meet even the minimum payment on its debt, and many foreign companies became nervous about investing in Mexico. An earthquake in 1985 caused mass destruction to parts of Mexico, and again the government was inadequate in its response. In the 1988 presidential election, suspicion of massive vote fraud led many Mexicans to denounce the entire political system.

By the early 1990s the economy of Mexico appeared on the verge of collapse. The value of the **peso** had dropped, while the prices of products were rising. However, the North American Free Trade Agreement (NAFTA) helped the economy of Mexico to grow. This agreement was negotiated between Mexico, the United States, and Canada in the early 1990s, and it removes trade restrictions and fees on imports and exports among these countries. The agreement provides opportunities for foreign companies to invest in Mexico, by making it less expensive for them to operate facilities there. Since the creation of NAFTA in

Rescue workers search the ruins of a building in Mexico City for survivors after a disastrous earthquake rocked the capital city in September 1985. The earthquake destroyed hundreds of buildings and killed at least 10,000 people.

1994, Mexico has signed free-trade agreements with many other countries, including China, Japan, the European Union, and many countries of Central and South America. Today, Mexico has the world's 14th-largest economy, with a gross domestic product (the value of all goods and services produced in a year) valued at over $1.3 trillion in 2014.

Despite this economic growth, Mexico remains a nation with significant problems. There is a huge gap between the wealthy and poor in the country, and many people live in squalid conditions. Roads and other public infrastructure are crumbling, and people in rural areas often have little access to electricity, clean

Mexico is the sixth-largest producer of oil in the world. Petroleum is a vital part of the Mexican economy, generating more than 10 percent of its export earnings.

drinking water, or public sewage. The educational system and the health care system are underfunded and overextended.

Unfortunately, violence continues to trouble Mexico. Since the mid-2000s Mexican authorities have been engaged in a brutal and bloody war against organized criminal gangs that are involved in smuggling illegal drugs into the United States. These gangs, known as drug cartels, are believed to control more than 90 percent of the illegal drugs smuggled into the United States today.

Many of the current drug cartels originated during the late 1980s, when a gangster named Miguel Ángel Félix Gallardo divided control over the key smuggling routes among his associates. A group called the Tijuana Cartel controlled all drug routes in the Mexican state of Baja California, including the Tijuana-San Diego border crossing. Control over smuggling routes around Ciudad Juárez, a city on the Rio Grande across from El Paso, Texas, was given to the Juárez Cartel headed by Rafael Aguilar Guajardo and brothers Amado and Vicente Carrillo Fuentes. Drug distribution from Sonora, a Mexican state that borders Arizona and New Mexico, was given to the Sonora Cartel, while shipment of drugs along the Gulf coast of Mexico, including the highly

populated border crossing area between Matamoros, Mexico, and Brownsville, Texas, was controlled by the Gulf Cartel. The trafficking of drugs from cities on Mexico's Pacific coast was given to an organization headed by two of Félix Gallardo's most trusted associates: Joaquín Guzmán Loera and Ismael Zambada García. Their organization became known as the Sinaloa Cartel.

The major Mexican drug cartels operated independently. Sometimes they

A Mexican soldier checks a vehicle for drugs at a checkpoint near Ciudad Juárez. Due to its position on the U.S. border, in 2009 and 2010 Ciudad Juárez was the most dangerous city in the world, with an extremely high murder rate.

Enrique Peña Nieto (right), president of Mexico, meets with U.N. Secretary-General Ban Ki-moon in Mexico City, April 2014. Peña Nieto's election in 2012 returned the PRI to power after a dozen years of PAN rule.

worked together; more often they fought with rival cartels to expand their operations. Any time a cartel leader died or was arrested, other groups would attempt to move in and take over that cartel's drug smuggling routes. Throughout the 1990s, the Mexican drug cartels gained power, and the government did little to stop them. In fact, the cartels would bribe local police officers and government officials to ignore their illegal activities.

Things began to change in 2000 with the election of Vicente Fox Quesada as president of Mexico. Fox represented Politico de Acción Nacional (PAN), a new political party that challenged the PRI, which had ruled Mexico for 70 years. President Fox was more willing than past leaders had been to work with the U.S. to prevent drug smuggling and illegal immigration. At the end of his term in office, he turned over a number of cartel leaders that Mexican authorities had arrested to the U.S. for trial.

Fox's successor as president, Felipe Calderón, would escalate the conflict with the cartels, known as the narco war. Soon after his election in 2006, Calderón ordered federal police and soldiers to intervene in the turf wars among the various cartels. This led to a sharp rise in violence, as gangsters engaged in shoot-outs with Mexican police.

When Calderón left office in 2012, his successor as president, Enrique Peña Nieto, promised to continue waging the narco conflict. To date, more than 80,000 people have been killed in drug-related violence, and Mexican federal police have arrested more than 120,000 people connected with cartels. However, despite government pressure and more than $1.5 billion in support from the United States, the narco war shows little sign of ending.

TEXT-DEPENDENT QUESTIONS

What is an ejido system?

Which president escalated the narco war by involving federal police and soldiers?

RESEARCH PROJECT

The North American Free Trade Agreement (NAFTA) is an agreement that eliminates tariffs and other barriers to trade and investment between the United States, Canada, and Mexico. At the time NAFTA was implemented in 1994, many people believed it would improve the standard of living for Mexican workers. Find out more about the agreement and its effect on Mexico's economy, and on the maquiladora system, over the past two decades. Which Mexican industries have benefited from NAFTA, and which have declined as a result of increased competition from foreign companies?

Pedestrians walk past the Monumento a la Revolución (Monument to the Revolution) in Mexico City. The monument is 220 feet (67 m) tall, and contains the remains of some of the most important revolutionary leaders, including former presidents Francisco Madero, Plutarco Elías Calles, Venustiano Carranza, and Lázaro Cárdenas.

SERIES GLOSSARY

adobe—a building material made of mud and straw.

Amerindian—a term for the indigenous peoples of North and South America before the arrival of Europeans in the late 15th century.

conquistador—any one of the Spanish leaders of the conquest of the Americas in the 1500s.

criollo—a resident of New Spain who was born in North America to parents of Spanish ancestry. In the social order of New Spain, criollos ranked above mestizos.

fiesta—a Mexican party or celebration.

haciendas—large Mexican ranches.

maquiladoras—factories created to attract foreign business to Mexico by allowing them to do business cheaply.

mariachi—a Mexican street band that performs a distinctive type of music utilizing guitars, violins, and trumpets.

Mesoamerica—the region of southern North America that was inhabited before the arrival of the Spaniards.

mestizo—a person of mixed Amerindian and European (typically Spanish) descent.

Nahuatl—the ancient language spoken by the Aztecs; still spoken by many modern Mexicans.

New Spain—name for the Spanish colony that included modern-day Mexico. This vast area of North America was conquered by Spain in the 1500s and ruled by the Spanish until 1821.

plaza—the central open square at the center of Spanish cities in Mexico.

pre-Columbian—referring to a time before the 1490s, when Christopher Columbus landed in the Americas.

FURTHER READING

Berdan, Frances F. *Aztec Archaeology and Ethnohistory*. London: Cambridge University Press, 2014.

Chávez, Alicia Hernández. *Mexico: A Brief History*. Berkeley: University of California Press, 2006.

Coe, Michael D., and Rex Koontz. *Mexico: From the Olmecs to the Aztecs*. New York: Thames and Hudson, 2008.

Franz, Carl, et al. *The People's Guide to Mexico*. Berkeley, Calif.: Avalon Travel Publishing, 2006.

Grillo, Ioan. *El Narco: Inside Mexico's Criminal Insurgency*. New York: Bloomsbury Press, 2011.

Gritzner, Charles F. *Mexico*. New York: Chelsea House, 2012.

Kent, Deborah. *Mexico*. New York: Children's Press, 2012.

Marley, David F. *Mexico at War: From the Struggle for Independence to the 21st-Century Drug Wars*. Santa Barbara, Calif.: ABC-CLIO, 2014.

Mayor, Guy. *Mexico: A Quick Guide to Customs and Etiquette*. New York: Kuperard, 2006.

Simon, Suzanne. *Sustaining the Borderlands in the Age of NAFTA: Development, Politics, and Participation on the US-Mexico Border*. Nashville: Vanderbilt University Press, 2014.

INTERNET RESOURCES

Mesoweb
http://www.mesoweb.com/welcome.html#externalresources

National Geographic
http://kids.nationalgeographic.com/kids/places/find/mexico

CIA World Factbook
https://www.cia.gov/library/publications/the-world-factbook/geos/mx.html

History of Mexico
http://www.history.com/topics/mexico

INEGI (Geographic, Demographic, and Economic Information of Mexico)
http://www.inegi.gob.mx/diffusion/ingles/portadai.html

Publisher's Note: The websites listed on this page were active at the time of publication. The publisher is not responsible for websites that have changed their address or discontinued operation since the date of publication. The publisher reviews and updates the websites each time the book is reprinted.

INDEX

63

PICTURE CREDITS

ABOUT THE AUTHOR

Amy N. Hunter is a writer from Ripley, West Virginia. She writes most frequently on business and technical matters but enjoys working on young adult pieces as well.